Tending Towards

Chaos

Tending Towards

Chaos

To Jay:
I hope you enjoy!

Ami Lovelace

Illustrations by Arianna Bruno

authorHOUSE®

AuthorHouse™
1663 Liberty Drive
Bloomington, IN 47403
www.authorhouse.com
Phone: 1-800-839-8640

First published by AuthorHouse   9/10/2010

ISBN: 978-1-4520-5414-8 (e)
ISBN: 978-1-4520-5412-4 (sc)
ISBN: 978-1-4520-5413-1 (hc)

Library of Congress Control Number: 2010912200

Printed in the United States of America

This book is printed on acid-free paper.

For all of my "Miracle Max"-es (or rather you're more like the wife of Miracle Max?) who helped me on my journey. Thank you for believing—this is for you.

Y para mi gente en Sevilla— os echo muchísimo de menos.

"-Do you think it will work?"
"-It would take a miracle!"

Special Thanks

I would like to thank the Academy (OK, just kidding, but I've always wanted to say that, and it's *my* book, so why not?). But, truly, this would not have been possible without the help and support of so many wonderful people throughout the years. I'd like to especially thank Jordyn for being my "tester", critiquing and encouraging in equal measure. Christine, for lighting a fire under my rear and pushing me to follow my dream— thank you. To Arianna Bruno for her wonderful illustrations and taking the time to collaborate with me on what I had envisioned. To Jenner Davis for making me look good, and keeping the shine off my "T-zone" with her amazing photography skills. To June, for her opinion, support, and encouragement. To B.—for being exactly who you are and for letting me learn from you. And to my mother, for everything, always.

Tending Towards

Chaos

Contents

Out of the darkness...

*P*art *I*

7.3

the quiet night's afire
alit with moon's organza veil
and the cloud's frothy tears work naught
to douse the sun's dwindling embers

stillness.

twilight's fingers gently outstretch
leaving heated caresses upon Earth's face
desire overwhelms deep in her nether core
a violent shudder bursting through to ecstatic release

eternal seconds.

and now breaking his silence
the breathless voyeur night howls
writhing to react in twists and moans
desperate to embrace a living entity

eruptive chaos.

I live on the fault line
and she has won over the night.

Elegy for the Gulf

Slick shine and bright swirls
black gold illuminates life
the sea is dying

Fiery rust swims
while pods rest on the beaches
choking on the air

Birds used to fly free
grounded and bathed now in blackness
feathers are poisoned

heavens' tears now fall
torrents disperse obsidian
Nature is mourning

Echoes of Rome

Tired and drained
the military mandated
strength stretched wide across the land
but what force left is there?

cities occupied,
pushing boundaries
Rome's mighty hand reaching, grasping

all focus outwards
expansion! expansion!—
implosion.
a praetorian? a marine?
one and the same?

corruption, bribes,
the Senate compromised
an Emperor greedy for power,
blinded by ambition,
he sits sipping nectar in his dove White tower.

Caesar was once ambitious, too
And Nero played while Rome burned
What, now, will this Emperor do?

For the Glory of the Media

Wield your guns
and take the plunge
it's time to celebrate
set it afire
build up the pyre
a rebellion we must create

let's break the pews,
and bask in the news
let's soak up all the fame
we must stage a scene
embrace the obscene
let's be swallowed by the flame

let's hunt down the young
take them out one by one
and revel in all the glory
we'll be homeward bound
just one more round
then be in all the news stories

San Francisco's Panhandle(r)

And the weeks march on,
Silent as the drum
And all you hear is their onward thrum
The people flurry to the rhythm of their beat
Revitalized and anxious- ne'er admit defeat
And so must I
Break the chain
Individualism and integrity to regain
I'll sit and watch
as they pass nigh
brainwashed sergeants at arms
and their corporate spies
I'd been one once
Not so long ago
now I hover on skid row
Begging now for small scraps
they said it was recession
which bled into Depression
checks to coins, and coins to crack
I barely think more than scoring smack
With my empty hand outstretched
The end is here, it's Friday at last
And all the soldiers of the week,
can kiss my ass.

Powell Street Station

And another.

Screeching metal resounds in the darkness
Howling brakes shriek under the strain of oppressing friction
And magnesium light convulses in epileptic fits
BART comes crashing to a halt

Confusion, panic, anger— the cars swell with emotion
Desperation smears its bloodied fragments upon the engine
And on the tracks
Mangled gore.
him or her— who now can tell?
and Rush Hour grinds to a stop

The whispers begin, initial screams now faded
lighted mini screens speckle the blackness
electronic stars shining in the dark
everyone will know soon—
the sound of buttons punctuate low murmurs

somber ambiance deflected by annoyance
thoughts reflected aloud
and the only words that echo down the cars
"I hope it's not delayed."

Street Chic

Compact held high she stares at herself
Slightly angling the mirror to ensnare the faintest ray of light,
an intensity in her countenance, brow arched
she softly strokes the contours of her eyelid
She wants to be beautiful,
and why shouldn't she? Is she not like the rest of us?

Acting nonchalant as I begin to glide by,
with an upheld head, I feign disinterest
all the while hoping my sunglasses do not
betray the wandrance of my gaze
She looks up at me, fingertips still fastening
the darkened brush to the crease of her eye
I am caught!

My neck stiffens and jilts, straining to seem aloof
my step quickens
unacquainted with such oddity
I am uncertain: is it acceptable to look? to notice?
or should this juxtaposition of beauty and homeliness not have
existed
to me?
to you?
to any passerby?

Who will look to her eyes to see the powdered lid?
Still, the bag lady continues to apply the make-up.

Urban Footprints

Shuffling down the concrete hall
stepping heavily, dragging bare toes
and yet, leaving no track at all
no memory to suffer their woes

eyes turned up, no path to follow
at 6am existence is swept away
no reminders of the souls so hollow
the trash collector has started his day

the gutter grapples with its loss
company and friend now gone
its tears flood heavy at the cost
this wretched, lonely dawn

dirty bedding, hard and cold
traded in for the sterile and pristine
on metal berth black rubber now enfolds
for a bum there is no mourning

Duality

It is your most cherished gift
your mortal curse
it is that thing you wrap your arms around
in a crushing embrace
trying to prevent it from slipping away

It is that nightmare you fear most
that dark shadow looming over you,
encroaching ever faster upon you

It is what you hope for, pray for
try to savor its taste
as it fleetingly teases your palate

It is what you avoid,
slither away from,
watch carefully from a safe distance
as it feeds on those around you

It brings you absolute pleasure,
hope, passion,
love

It brings you sadness,
disappointment, pain
heartbreak

in that instant
when the Time comes

Sun and Shade

ritual steeped in myth
pagan veins conquered by the riches of Christianity
then given over to the vulgar
yet, it survives
pageantry, artistry
the years have wrought
And yet, it is untainted
Pomp and precision admired still

Russets, black, ochre and blues
the colors that dance under the sun
persuaded through the rhythmic twirls
and the dips of an ancient waltz

a bailarín in his finest regalia
vivid shades blend in an artist's swirl
reflecting in the glimmer of the master's gold
entrancing as he moves around the circle

Ah! But what lays underneath?
Scars of his passion speckle his form
fears manifested into truths, memories
And yet, he maneuvers still
an old face with a young heart
performing. Dancing.
a three part masterpiece

Flashes of gold caught in the sun's eye
a box step and a spin, partners in a twirl
flowing, billowing
artistry on display,

With brass horns rejoicing, and a rhythmic stutter
the spectacle is drawing to an end
then a flash of the mighty and a mistake of the weak
and—
with no applause, no petition for reward
his fans have fallen silent
the bull has won this afternoon
the Macarena, now, is crying.

Image contributed by Ami Lovelace

Fear

it is ruthless, unforgiving
a dark shadow that surrounds the soul
engulfs the heart
tortures the mind
it is indiscriminate,
loathing,
feeding upon emotions
 it is a deterrent
from happiness, from truth
from freedom

Fear
it is irrational, chaotic
a swirling tempest raging in full fury
it is sleeplessness
a starless night with no known dawn,
it is the nightmares,
bloodcurdling screams,
heart-stopping breathlessness

Fear
it is controlled, thoughtful
a calculating enemy
it is all powerful
self-perpetuating
self-assured
it is a weapon
a tyrannical dictator
a war

Fear— it holds me captive

Jungle Canopy

out on a branch
she dangles
alone, gripping tightly
clinging, holding on

she'd gone out there,
ventured past her comfort zone,
and now she dangles,
dangles all alone

her fingers gripping,
clenching tightly
scared to death of falling

blood writhes down her hand
dripping, dripping slightly
scared to death of falling

Pretense

there's a safety in your arms,
a warm comfort that I long for,
can't get enough of,
yet I fear it,
afraid you'll take it away

your whispers are soft, sweet,
reassuring
meant to smooth away my tears,
and yet you don't know,
your words are their cause
I cry for their loss

Purgatory

alone she waits,
it's half past eight
listening for the phone
it's a Friday night
she's not in sight
home, hand clasped upon her phone

she waits to hear
his voice in fear
wondering what he'll say
she prays he'll call
that they'll get past it all
and hopes that he will stay

she dwells on the end
wonders if it began
afraid that she will lose
she let herself fall
broke down her own walls
and now waits to let him choose

Jaded Kaleidoscope

Colored spots and polka dots,
she sees them spinning preen,
love marooned with bitter wounds
but soon she licks them clean
Salted cries and bitter lies
she's been through it all before
stomach rot and love forgot
she'll hear of it no more
Wayward pratter and bedside flatter
subduing her anger for now
she's radiant not ignorant
she too has been on the prowl.

But She Had Said No

she stood alone in a window
watching the sunrise
gazing unseeingly at the horizon
the sparkle dulling in her eyes

her thoughts buzzing in a whir
as tears silently skidded down her face
she was lost in her own darkness
floundering in disgrace

tainted and ashamed
writhing in her own skin
she shivers reliving the nightmare
still taking it all in

disbelief dissolves
and anger is cast aside
while despair begins to set in
she has no where to hide

over and over it replays
the monsters in her bed
and while he moves on to flirt with the next
she'll never get him out of her head

the persistent, disgusting bastard
she'll never let it go
most of her life she'll blame herself
even though she had told him, "NO!"

The Rotted Seed

Hateful, wretched man.
Why dost thou terrify so
Under iron hand, oppression reigns,
gilded in tarnishing gold
Childish flagrancy
Love thy self—
no son shall live to bear your name
as many are accursed,
wasting in glittered decadence
so shall you wither,
in a whore's spiteful luxury
with putrefying pomegranates
ever faithful in your palm
and then decay prevails
ripe upon your skin
as lingering as your courtly conquests
and while discretion gives way,
ne'er your better part of valor
death becomes the harbinger of revival
a fete of bloodlust anointed by pious hand

The Last Dance on the Card

The old man reached for his partner
wrinkled hand and weathered face timid
fingertips trembling in expectation, and age
the wintry eve closing soon on his cotillion

Ah how light he once had been
nimble, spry, the jovial movements of his youth
but, transformed joints now emblems of Celtic knots
entwined in arthritic pain
and yet, determination breathes briefly,
new life to a stagnant body
his card is full and he intends to dance to the end

Around and around they glide, encircling the floor,
a dizzying psychedelic experience for the eyes
yet he refuses to close them
not yet
defiance keeps him looking on
the shapes and shades blending into recognition
then memories

yet now the music slows,
beat whirring down to a softened thrum
gentle vibrations releasing the body's captive energy

and his mistress, pale and beautiful,
black dress lifting gently in the final twirl
a sensual play to excite the echo of an old man's heart
before he stops—to dip her
he hesitates not, for one last passionate kiss
gulping down the taste of life
and a final expiration settles him into rest
back in the hospital bed
his dance with Death has come to an end

Letters from the Grave

To a friend,
    with all my love

I want to see your smiles, and the sparkle in your eyes. I want to hear your laughter, not your sorrows nor your cries. I want to see your face brighten, with every joke that's made. I want to see your personality grow, and the warmth in you never fade. I want to see you enjoy life, never regret a single day. I want to see you move on, and all your pain tossed away. Yes, dear friend, my body is still, but I will remain in your heart. And because of this you should know, from you my spirit will never part.

In closing, my sweet love, I ask you to promise me just one thing:

To live your life to the fullest, and always let your heart sing. Please, dear friend, do not cry, it's time now to say good-bye. And though I know it's hard to say, please wipe all your tears away.

Eaters of the Dead

The faces of the dead floating around us
Souls ferried in the darkness
lantern lit, Charon collecting
Styx—roaring, churning,

Disappearing in the distance
forgotten, but not gone
ancestors sins reverberating the halls
heirlooms to lay at the hands of progeny
Hades will have disciples

Eaten. Eaten. Swallowed by the earth.
By the nothingness.

Widow's Countenance.

her blue eyes tell
old and fading,
her words— a shell,
of the story she's masquerading

in her blank gaze,
solitude screams,
each hair that strays,
broadcasts interrupted dreams

her seeds of desire
long since gone,
twenty years buried
in Laurel Grove lawn

the milky web
spun across her eye
catches the tears that fall
alone when she cries

she speaks now and then
when no one's near
reminiscing with an empty rocking chair
her Soul now disappeared

Positive

Drawing in breath
She speaks through trembling lips
gnawing nervously
eyes fighting, beseeching through the tears
this may just kill her,
more so, worse even, than *it* will.
but forward is the only way to go.
forward and on. She must.
truth, fear, loathing, anxiety, anger.
Confession.
It pours from what had once been sweet, supple, inviting lips.
Now tainted, dirty and disgusting. Diseased.
crawling in her own skin
how does she soothe *him*? steady *him*? protect *him*?
convince *him* to stay...
She is not the enemy. Not to him.
but how, now, to touch him? To stave off unwarranted guilt,
Not contaminate.
withdrawing, her soul pulls back, hovering in shadows
terrified of pain
not the pain *it* will cause her. No.
His.

Calloused palms hoist Yesterday's memories

Calloused palms hoist Yesterday's memories
Unrecognized faces blurring in Scenes
a love of younger days burns wildly
Time is ending

Drowning souls whispered

Drowning souls whispered
Listen to confessions
Plunging tormented souls
condemned desperation
ungodly addiction masks obsessions
warning screams
then mutilated silence
and
broken love

Pursuing Lore

and love goes
threading its existence into the framework of my story quilt
a trail of bread crumbs left for voracious pursuants
and leading to the fiery oven?
if you stop believing, close your eyes and count—
does it exist? Still? before your eyes?
To antagonize, threaten, terrify?
or does the wingèd boogeyman become a figment
lost in the dregs of imagination?

leaving the spectral resonance
a ghostly chill that wrenches the guts, crawls up the spine
reminding you of something—
—of nothing, you should long to recall
So,
Adolescence wrests the monsters from reality
Grotesque demons morphed, while,
innocence, lost, banishes the unicorn
and the Cerynian Hind hunted down.

if you cease to hope
what then to live for, aspire to?
does that, too, wither into the shades of nonexistence?
for one person? for all?
So who then forfeits love?
Gives up on believing the myth? to lay aside the quest?
The weak? the warrior?

either way, not me.
Penelope unweaves to weave again.
The lore woven into my existence.
No. Not me.

The Horned Creature of the Night

Bare boned, exposed
He shivers,
a tingling numbness begins to consume him
reaching its fingers,
frosty nails lightly gliding through his core
countering his heat
he writhes, twitching and toes curling,
powerless to the sensation
the oppositions of elements:
pleasing summer and repellant winter dancing over his skin
glistening beads leave reflecting pools
dotted along their uplifted path
shuttering now, his breath quickens, desperate
oh how he fights, struggles with the fiend that gorges upon him
white-fleshed and vulnerable, the man will lose
the beast hungers tonight

Eternal seconds strike
unable and now unwilling to dislodge
but desirous of release
final expiration escapes in violent ecstasy
he collapses, darkness entrapping his eyes, body shuttering then
still
the feeding frenzy is over

For tonight.

Ablutions

her warm streaming tears—
　　—lost in the heated droplets pounding on her face
emotions caught in a whirlpool, circling then disappearing
trying to wash away the hurt
never once refusing her
never turning cold to usher her out
allowing her to be herself, for as long as she needed,
huddled in the warm embrace

she would stifle gasps, cry out,
nakedly baring a lacerated soul
never speaking, never judging,
just listening,
comfortingly soothing, caressing her candidness
it was her sanctuary

it's been over a year
she doesn't cry in the shower anymore
she is healed

The Phoenix

There we were
food spread out
sitting Shivah, in mourning
I watched her,
tear-stricken face, flushed and shining
we sat there shrouded in loss,
in death
she grieved, broken-hearted
water crystals forming on her eyelashes
and I sat vigil, astute and aware
for what she did not know,
for what she could not see—

it was not his death we were grieving,
it was her own
she herself had passed,
never again to be the same person—
her soul had died
and although she did not realize it
her tears had become fallen ashes
the droplets of her former self
flecking away the final bits of a tortured soul
gathering and awaiting the time
when she, as does the Phoenix,
will rise again,
a new person,
mended and whole.

Porcelain

Sometimes she wishes she were porcelain-like
breakable, beautiful
esteemed in value,
and handled with gentleness
something to be put on a shelf—
admired

maybe a doll, with painted-perfect eyes,
rosy cheeks, and cherry lips
the paragon of beauty
or
delicate bone china
perfectly hand-painted and reflective
a gift of newly-wedded hope

Oh, to be an investment
the pride of her collector
the envy of the setting
Adored.

Never played with.
Never tossed aside.
Whole. Pure. Protected.
Frozen in perfection
A pleasing, porcelain piece.

Dreary Days

a
grey sky
is a limitless wonder

a vast unknown to be shaped,
moulded, imagined

feared and loved
it has a role
of both a cloak and a revealer
an opportunity lost...
...and gained

folding and unfolding
wrapping in itself
swallowing lives of those who
rest under it

it is a Mystic
left for us to perceive it as we will
Let us choose our own destiny!

Out of the Darkness

Out of the darkness
in the depths of the mind
lay creatures that wait
across spaces and time

Our souls fight the demons
the epic battles ensue
alone in the obscurity
afraid we might lose

But we champion on
what choice is there?
resilience and courage
against fear and despair

Hidden from view
the war wages on
internal judgments
sacrifices drawn

and then one day
only one fighter's left
the mind has quieted
voices bereft

and as victors we stand
in all the glory and might
stepping out of the darkness
And into the light

...And into the light

Part II

Awaiting the gold sphere

Awaiting the gold sphere
astral light fades
Apollo's archer banishes Morpheus
And morrow's weaver spins a deep love for two.

With the arrival of the golden chariot
heat rises to awaken Eros' kiss
and the lovers tremble in Decadence
caught in the glimmering haze

Eos

and the golden sparkle of morning's eye
lifts its gaze above the lavender pillowed mountains
alerted now to the sounds of wakefulness
avian songs energize in soothing alarm
calling her forth from the cradle of Morpheus

eagerness abated, converted to slow steady kinetics
rising from her soft slumber

early yoga inspires the ascension
a long, plotted stretch augments her radiance
now shining high, bright and full
she glows- a happy luminescence
casted upon those within her gaze
and warmed by her presence

The Gift Within

To fear and to love
To watch and to wait
As the moments press on
Time seals our fate.

To love one another
As only we can
And to feel the emotion
In the touch of one's hand

The complexity of feelings
That make us all whole
Guarded under layers
Within the depths of the soul.

And the flame that ignites us
With a passion that roars
Driving us forward
Burning from our core

This entity dwelling inside us
we oft wonder what it could be
it's one of the greatest gifts we have—
It's our humanity.

Lifetime

How do you measure a lifetime?
is it the number of smiles we share
in the tears we shed
or in the number of sighs that escape our lips?

Do we count the echoes of laughter?
the resounding tremor of fear
or the times we've mended the pieces of our shattered hearts?

Do we number the wrinkles imprinted upon our skin?
the bones we have broken
or the characteristic scars we either hide or wear with honor?

Is a lifetime measured in the wishes blown on candles
or whispered upon shooting stars
or by the ever faithful moon we look to in the darkest of nights

A lifetime—
my lifetime
cannot be measured
but for those moments experienced next to you.

Persistent Soldier

Storm the sandy beaches
Climb the jagged crags
Reach the mountain's summit
and there you'll plant your flag

With a soldier's pride and honor
to the front lines you depart
Conquering a mighty battlefield
Steadfast always is your heart

Weather-worn you wear your armor,
Weapon ready at your side
Battle anxious in the trenches
no where to run and hide

The signal has been given
The first strike has begun
Adrenaline pulsates through you
Will your victory be won?

You've seen others fall before you
Wrecked and wounded beyond repair
Bleeding they lay broken
the field drenched with their despair

You advance dodging mortars
Bullets screaming past your head
Fear does not overcome you
Courage and determination keep your tread

The enemy's ranks are breaking
the lines are in retreat
the fortifications begin to crumble
Your enemy soon admits defeat

Your win is laden in lush riches
Banner waving o'er the conquered ramparts
Stake your claim in this new land
that which is my heart.

Parisian Moonlight

A bluish lavender color,
Encasing the darkened sky
Speckles of the silvered moon
in the reflection of your eye

A burst of warmth emitting
exuding from your enamored smile
the soothing of your words
spoken softly in a romantic's style

And as we stroll among the streets
the blood pulsates through my veins
In the city made for lovers
our feelings are the same.

Giddy—to the top of the tower we flee
entranced by the charming sights
and then I lose myself in your tender kiss
under the soft Parisian moonlight.

Drifting ecstasy

Drifting ecstasy
scattered Dreams
delicious emotion
blending beings
dancing Images
wispy desires
tempting love
unrestrained fires

Silvered Memories pardoned

Silvered Memories pardoned
the ghostly silence
Naked Feelings and countless heartaches
Freed lost lovers
love's hope Found their Wounded Souls.

Where light stages the stardust

Where light stages the stardust
and solar bursts dance
As playful fingers embrace Time
They find our love

You reached Out to stars

You reached Out to stars
laughed at the moon
desiring love for lifetimes
and Found Me.

She desired loving Souls

She desired loving Souls,
and found hardened Words,
She longed for memories.
you apologized softly,
missing Her.

Your heart beat

Your heart beat,
pressed sweetly against me
Love's timeless passion smiled
as your soft lips tickled my cheek
your love held me close.

Morning Reverie

Your scent,
it lingers on my skin
A blissful tingle to a morning's marathon
reverberating off my body
even as the memories of you wash over me in waves
Ah, delight!
A serving to my thoughts,
a delectable appetizer to stave off passion's hunger
Breathlessly stealing a moment's inhale,
taking in the slight echoes of your essence
I could not wash you away, even if I wanted to.

Garden

Look here iron rose
Gaze not upon the sunflower
for she will turn her glance upward

Make use the garden moon
Soften your steely petals
for pollination cannot occur in a closed bud

Hold high your gentle bloom
Tear not upon Morning's arrival
for she is cool and crisp with all

Stand proud upon your rigid stem
But mind me, the dirt, at your feet below
for here I am to nourish you
and you need me—
need me to grow.

Caught Up

So afraid to lose
Strung up on
a broken noose
We'll party high like we have all night
But in the end we'll do what's right
Lovers happy in their prime
At the beginning we run out of time
Then it's a flash-bang right to the pan
Throw sizzle to the fire and seek a different man

Watch the playful fox belie
The pirate's captured my good eye
Be wary in guarding my treasure chest
Gold pieces shattered in innocent jest
Off I'm whisked across the open sea
Wind carrying the tune of the siren's plea

Souls lost in two blue swirls
Hands tied up in rustic curls
Pandora's come to unlatch the chain
Yet in my box still hope remains.

Meditation

The inner peace of solitude
lifts lightly up my soul
tranquil blues and serene greens
massage soothingly
eyes closed
deep breaths in meditation
one side then the next
cleansing out the darkness
releasing all the stress

relaxation ebbs and flows
as the lavenders begin
elevating the harmonies
and then tingling on my skin

waves now of pale pinks
a kaleidoscope of pleasure
calm energy deepens into stillness
and nothing then to treasure

Discovering El Camino

500 free miles
the road so daunting
weaving spirits with lives
and so the path is calling

16 stone steeled kinetics
trudging through til dawn
defying natured challenge
down the Camino moving along

in seeking inner wisdom
solitude it provides
while yet teeming with life
throughout the Spanish countryside

royalty, priests— warriors alike
all sharing the pilrgim's journey
echoes of history reverberate
breathing life into their stories

enlightenment and fulfillment
the breeze carries evolution on her breath
and so we morph along the way
souls reborn only after their death

Image contributed by Ami Lovelace

Nostalgia's Village

Settling in,
it is a vision of ease, and comfort,
as familiar and soothing as the giggling of a babe,
treading feet dancing lightly on its mother's belly

its absence is draining, ourselves lost without it
we long to return, are drawn to its power
nestling into its warm caress
falling heartily, embraced by its welcoming outstretched arms

we stray, yet it is unconditional,
it awaits our coming
rising to stand on the horizon
when we again turn our eyes again upon it

we take advantage, turn away
and abandon without thought
and yet, still, it reaches to comfort us

That Girl on the Road

Introduce me to myself
Look into the eyes of the young woman staring back
Do you recognize?
Do you see who I am?
Do you see who she is?
Stare hard and long at the woman blinking back
She comes along, every once in while, with a glint in her iris
I know she knows

She dares to hope
and lives to dream
and all the while she is who she seems
fearful and fearless, a mystery and a memory
a nostalgic comfort
She has learned to lead with her heart and follow with her head
To speak through her soul and listen with her breath
She touches with her eyes
and smiles through her touch
all the while knowing
and she knows I know—

She is me, and I've found her again and at last.

Just Me

I'll never be that woman
most men fantasize about
the one with long legs and perfect curves
with a supermodel's pout

I'll never be a natural blonde
nor have a cocoa butter tan
you'll never see me in the swimsuit issue
or making love to a camera in the sand

I'll never have those perfect thighs
nor eyes just like the sea
I'm not the portrait of a Greek goddess
Cause, baby, that's just me,

I will, however, flash a smile
when something clever comes my way
and you'll always hear my resounding laughter
reacting to the entertaining things you say

I'll bat my lashes and flirt a bit
and quite possibly make you blush
I'll tempt you and I'll tease you
And to my bed you'll rush

I'll carry myself with pride
true class and dignity
I'll show you real character and brilliance
Cause, baby, that's just me

You'll never want to leave my side
experiencing such different beauty
I'll make you want to fall in love
Cause, baby, that's just me.

Pandora's Box

She peeks around the corner
wonder in her eyes
there ahead she sees it
her spirits start to rise

 She creeps up slowly towards it
ever gently- handling with care
cautious not to approach too quickly
praying it won't disappear

She pushes herself onward
wary of any misstep
working up her courage
not wanting to seem inept

Captivated by it
she's nervous reaching out
is it really there for her?
she struggles with the doubt

Her fingers slightly graze it
excitement takers her over
hesitation slows her pace
yet still she moves in closer

She can't believe she has it
something she'd rarely dreamt of
yet now she holds it close and dear,
this little thing called love.

To a Mother, from a Child

Momma, Momma,
if I died tomorrow,
would you be proud of me?

Would there be a smile in your loving eyes
as they filled with saddened tears?

Momma, Momma,
if I died tomorrow,
would you be proud of me?

Would there be a happiness,
filling every bittersweet memory of me
that lingered in your head?

Momma, Momma,
if I died tomorrow,
would you be proud of me?

Would there have been
more things you wanted from me,
things I didn't do good enough?

Momma, Momma
if I died tomorrow,
would you be proud of me?

Would I go to heaven mommy?
Would you leave me if I went?
Would you still love me, Momma?

To a Child, from a Mother

Oh, my child,
I will always be proud of you,
no matter when death comes and holds your hand.

My red eyes would burn
with fiery love, always smiling,
through the tears

My sweet child,
I will always be proud of you
no matter when death comes and holds your hand

My sorrowful soul would
be filled with a contentedness
only you could make

My precious love,
I will always be proud of you
no matter when death comes and holds your hand

There is nothing I could ask from you,
that would have made me happier—
you are my child

My dear baby,
I will always be proud of you
no matter when death comes and holds your hand

Heaven would welcome you lovingly,
but they'd have to take me too—
For if you were to go,
then a piece of me would too
That's the kind of love I have for you,
Unconditional, pure and true.

It only takes a moment

it only takes a moment
to spread a smile across your face
to meet someone's eye
to brighten a stranger's day

it only takes a moment
to lend a compassionate ear
to extend a loving touch
to give comfort through embrace

it only takes a moment
to share in a fit of laughter
to chase a lover in play
to kiss away a tear

it only takes a moment
to create a lasting memory
to leave an imprint on a soul
to tell someone you love them

it only takes a moment.

live the moments you are given
brighten lives if you are willing
because, it only takes a moment
to lose someone

The Bliss of Fire

I ask them why
And they answer
"We have fallen."
And I wonder:
   "as the Angels had?"
but, No.
 In this, Grace is magnified.
        They are lifted. Elevated.
Higher than their past selves could ever have been
Better than they could ever have been.
No, they have not fallen.
Love is a choice. A decision—
To accept. Respect
To care—equally. More.
      For the other.
It is forever.
the fire that is lit
     —an eternal flame.
inescapable.
Sometimes raging—
     Passionate, bright, and engulfing
Other times dwindling—
     Embers small and smoldering
But most times it is a tamed flame—
     Constant, crackling, yet controlled.
And it burns always,
    to comfort
    to keep the warmth in the coldest of moments

No—they did not fall.
Not into the fire.
They chose it—together.

Tending Towards Chaos

And looking at the stars
the galaxy stretched,
Miles away, and beyond the darkness
swirling colors to encircle
embracing her
the girl stood,
precipice plunging from her feet
and soaring— vast opportunity
dancing before her
a lifted sea
calm in vision yet churning and tempestuous in its depths
dizzying microcosms
life, centrifugally bound
one to the other, though never touching
dreams twinkle in the distance
consuming black holes feed on
chaotic aspirations—
leaving
paradoxical traces: both nothing and something
force ebbs and flows, energy recycled
back into the girl's hands
creativity restrained by— by nothing.
Gravity is mastered.

Viene una vagabunda mundial

*P*arte III

¡Y Olé!

Me crecí desde fuera
pero ni siquiera me siento extranjera
porque soy de Sevilla
de la corona a la patita
De mi barrio Triana
y de mi parroquia Santa Ana
Sangro verdiblanco
y conozco a aquel nazareno del Altozano
Toco las palmas
y bailo Sevillanas
Sé bien quién es la Pantoja
y he comido la milhoja
Voy a las corridas de toros
y por el puente he visto cruzar el Cachorro
mi Virgen Madre es la Esperanza
la más guapa de todo Triana
y el Cristo de las Tres Caídas
delante de quien me pongo de rodillas
Porque soy Carmen la de Triana
y aunque sea americana
Soy andaluza y sevillana,
¡y más TRIANERA que ná!

Las Cosas de Triana

Las cosas de Triana:
Nuestra Madre la Esperanza
quien mira por sus fieles
en la oscuridad de la madrugada

y el Cristo de San Gonzalo
que al parecer caminando
regresa para su gente
en su recogida por el Altozano

y por los llantos de la Estrella
que por la noche nos rodean
al entrar en su capilla
siempre nos inspiran la saeta

y Nuestro Padre de la muerte
no hay una imagen más fuerte
que el Santísimo Cristo del Cachorro
con sus nazarenos por el puente

y por nuestra calle Castilla
se sitúa una capilla
en que se alberga la Virgen de la O
con toda su cara joven y fina

A La Barrera

Es la hora
y se van cayendo
Qué bravos y guapos fueron
pero ya se van falleciendo

Es el arte de la vida
La danza de la muerte
A ver cuál es él que superará
Cuál es él que será el fuerte

La lucha es más que ves
No ves los demonios que los amenazan
Encerrados con sus miedos
Siempre ante la Macarena ellos rezan

Hay que ver sus caras tan jóvenes
Sus cuerpos de buen físico
En ellos los trajes pintados
Sus almas algo místico

"!Que tenga suerte hijo!"
reza un mayor
antes de eso momento
que para todos menos uno, es el mejor.

La Intimidad de Anochecer

un alma desnuda
frente al anochecer
un corazón suplicando
el momento para extender
una mujer sencilla
a tu mirar
una palabra susurrada
un deseo para saciar
un roce estimulante
la esperanza de repetir
una cara ruborizando
la verdad aún para decir
una pasión ardiente
a momentos de estallar
un amor escondido
al punto de contar
una confesión femenina
se acaba de saber
tras un beso bienvenido
no tienes que responder

Prisionera

Quítame las cadenas me has puesto
Libérame mi juicio encarcelado
Déjame con lo que queda
un corazón por ti condenado

Suéltame mis sentimientos secuestrados
Devuélveme mi tiempo quitado
Permíteme superar a lo que pueda
de todos mis recuerdos destrozados

Sécame las lagrimas penosas
Entrégame la felicidad perdida
Restáurame la capaz que me cedas,
pá volver a vivir mi propia vida

Quítale los esposos de las manos,
Ábrele la gran puerta cerrada,
Suéltale del encierro desgraciado,
¡que no se muera la prisionera abandonada!

el Niño del Parque

el mundo para descubrir
grande— todo para conseguir
un parque— su paraíso
un árbol— su desafío
tan enorme le parece todo
un mar de diversiones sin fondo
momentos se convierten en horas
todo el desconocido explora
no existe ni una gota de miedo
ni piensa en el riesgo
saluda a los visitantes
una alegría en su semblante
se sienta al lado mío
mirándome con curiosidad el crío
se levanta y se va
corre a la próxima novedad
se tira pá allá y pá acá
lanzándose encima de su papá
por el parque su risa resuena
hasta el oscurecer el chiquitín juega
mi inspiración ya se va
acompañado por su papá
su inocencia aún protegida
y por eso le tengo envidia

Tus Virtudes

Tienes una manera de amarme
que me cautiva el corazón
expresas una ternura al mirarme
que en mi alma causa una explosión

En tu risa se escucha la inocencia
que me lleva a mi niñez
en tus susurros se presenta la paciencia
que me saca de la timidez

Muestras una dulzura al acariciarme
que en mí provoca la pasión
me proporcionas una confianza al hablarme
que afianza nuestra relación

Me seduce tu inteligencia
aunque la disimulas en tu sensatez
me impresiona tu decencia
eres mi caballero de la honradez

Haces que quiera mejorarme
has sido mi bendición
y por eso a ti quiero entregarme
sin sentir ninguna aprensión

La Otra

Amigo mío, disgustao
Te di mi corazón
Te di me mano
Te daría lo que fuera,
Sólo para verte sonreír
Pero ya nos llega la hora
En la que nos tenemos que despedir
Tus ojos brillantes me han guiao
En los tiempos más oscuros
Tu alma radiante ha sido mi faro
Siempre te buscaba
Navegando por la vida
Pero ya me has abandonado
Dejándome sobrevivir sólita

La muerte nunca es justa
solo cuidase a si misma
No da ni razón ni excusa
Ni nos pide nuestra perdón
y así, ¿por qué le has decidío perseguirla?
Con el egoísmo que tiene
Sabías que nunca podías elegirla—

Sin perderte a mí

El Sólo

Se pone alto y orgulloso
Por los dedos de sus rayos dorados y brillantes
ella le da de comer
todo lo que tiene,
todo lo que es suficiente.

pero, todavía él sigue solo,
ella le sopla el pelo
con su aliento ligero y suave
pero no responde
simplemente se queda temblando

Suavemente le susurra
sobre amigos desde mucho fallecidos
lo acaricia con su mano
jugando con los hilos salvajes
pero sus intereses están repetidos

nada lo rodea, solo quien ser
le coge todo lo que pueda
ese árbol tan piadoso
Y qué le da a ella?
La palmera le das su belleza

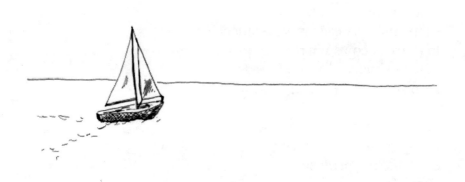

Esclava al Mar

Yo soy capitána de un barco
que no para de navegar
Tu eres el horizonte
a que nunca puedo llegar
marcas mi camino
y sigo siempre pá delante
mientras te burlas de mí
quedándote fuera de mi alcance
eres el punto de mi mundo más importante
donde mi cielo se encuentra con mi mar
donde las nubes calmantes con sus caricias
hacen las olas tormentosas suavizar
he vagado por todas las aguas
la ancla de mi nave sin descansar
desesperada para llegar a tu Puerto mítico
y para mi gran sueño marinero alcanzar

El Deseo

Abre tus ojos
aquí estoy mi amor
te ofrezco lo todo
mi corazón, mi alma... mi calor

Mírame los ojos
ve que no te miento
los deseos caprichosos
por y para ti siento

Daría la misma vida
pá estar siempre a tu lao
pá nunca sufrir tu perdida
pá nunca verte desdichao

Ven A Mi, Señor

Ven.
Quiero que vengas a mi.
Dame Tu luz, Tu amor Tu gracia.
Ahora, luego, siempre.
Quiero sentir que estas conmigo
cada mañana, cuando me levanto
durante el día y cada noche,
antes de dormirme
sin dejar de estar a mi lado
se que estas conmigo
ya lo se
Te quedas en mi corazón
para que Te guarde, Te recuerde
Te quiera, siempre
Para que yo sepa que Tu me quieres.

En Camino Contigo

Oh que tenga Tus palabras!
Tu voluntad!
Que me refleje en Ti.
Me has cambiado
Me estas cambiando
Te busco, Te espero, Te necesito
Que hagas a través de mi, Tus obras
Mis manos son Tuyas, condúcelas.
Mis pies son Tuyos, hazlos andar
Mi boca es Tuya, echa por ella la Palabra
Mi corazón es Tuyo, llénalo con Tu amor
Mi espíritu viene de Ti, que brille para que Te vean
En camino siempre, guiada por ti.

Le Contesté

Me llamó un día,
yo estaba en Triana,
vino a mi puerta,
cuando me paraba en Triana.
Se la abrí, y le escuché,
cada Palabra que me decía,
y más se lo creía,
cada sentimiento sentirme hacía.
Me dijo que lo siguiera,
pero más lo perseguí,
y caminamos por Triana,
hacia la Santa Ana de allí.
Ay mi madre Santa Ana,
con sus hijos, buenos pastores,
me guiaron para conocerlo,
al Señor de los señores.
Bajó a la Pila de los Gitanos,
donde se quedó siempre conmigo,
y me convirtió en Su hija Carmen,
para ser siempre Su testigo.

El Faro

Que brille yo en la oscuridad,
Que vengan a mí,
pero a mí, no
a Tu Luz, Señor
Que vengan a Tu luz,
que ilumina todo
Que es el faro de la vida
que ama a todos
Que vengan a mí, Señor
Porque Te vean a ti.

Sus Palabras en Mis Dedos

Mis pozos guardan
Su agua
Su vida, mi vida,
son inseparables
y El deja que la saque
para los que la necesitan
Que necesitan a Él
y Él
Siempre me rellena los pozos
Nunca me falta nada
Nunca me falta Él.

About the Author

Photography by Jenner Davis

Ami Lovelace is the quintessential modern vagabond. Born in Pennsylvania, and not one to let grass grow under her feet, she has pursued her dreams across continents and oceans, having lived in several US cities and resided two years in Seville, Spain, she now finds herself currently anchored in San Francisco, California. Ami spent her undergraduate years at Gettysburg College in Pennsylvania, where she earned a B.A. in Spanish Language and Literature, with a dual minor in Classical Studies and Political Science (International Relations). An intrepid learner in life, Ami is actively looking to pursue a M.F.A. in Creative Writing while concurrently working on her first fiction novel and a collection of non-fiction short stories based on her quirky travel experiences. She writes with sage wisdom through a young heart.

Visit the Official Website of Ami Lovelace at www.amilovelace.com or her Facebook FanPage www.facebook.com/amilovelace.writer Follow Ami on Twitter: @amilovlace

LaVergne, TN USA
22 September 2010
198086LV00002B/43/P